Rules! Rules! Rules!

Malcolm Munene and Kyra Ostendorf

Illustrated by Steve Mark

Library of Congress Cataloging-in-Publication Data
Names: Munene, Malcolm, author. | Ostendorf, Kyra, author. | Mark, Steve, illustrator.
Title: Rules! rules! rules! / Malcolm Munene and Kyra Ostendorf ; illustrated by Steve Mark.
Description: Minneapolis, MN : Free Spirit Publishing, an imprint of Teacher Created Materials, Inc., 2023. | Series: Little laugh & learn | Audience: Ages 6–9
Identifiers: LCCN 2022037180 (print) | LCCN 2022037181 (ebook) | ISBN 9781631987229 (paperback) | ISBN 9781631987236 (ebook)
Subjects: LCSH: Social norms—Juvenile literature. Classification: LCC GN493.3 .M86 2023 (print) | LCC GN493.3 (ebook) | DDC 306—dc23/eng/20220920
LC record available at https://lccn.loc.gov/2022037180
LC ebook record available at https://lccn.loc.gov/2022037181

Edited by Eric Braun
Cover and interior design by Colleen Pidel
Illustrated by Steve Mark

Printed in China

Free Spirit Publishing
An imprint of Teacher Created Materials
9850 51st Avenue North, Suite 100
Minneapolis, MN 55442
(612) 338-2068
help4kids@freespirit.com
freespirit.com

Rules!
Rules!
Rules!

CONTENTS

LISTEN
NO
YES
HURRY UP
SHHHHH
QUIET!
SPEAK UP

So Many Rules!

Have you ever thought about all the rules you have to follow? There are so many!

Rules are part of your day from morning to night. You probably have rules . . .

- at school
- at home
- with your friends
- for screen time
- for bedtime
- for all the time—Sheesh!

Some rules are easy to understand.

That makes sense. It keeps you safe!

Some rules you probably do without even thinking.

You've had that rule since you were little. No one has to tell you anymore. It's automatic!

Some rules you are still learning to follow. Maybe you have a pet you help care for. You're learning what they need and the rules for helping out.

Do This. Don't Do That.

All these rules! It can make a person want to scream.

Of course, you know screaming won't help. In fact, it will probably just make more trouble. What *will* help? Understanding the reasons for rules.

Knowing the reasons for rules can help you remember them. And it can help you feel good about following them. Rules can make life smoother and easier for you—and for other people too.

That's what this book is all about.

And here's a **bonus**. Following rules can also lead to more independence. What does that mean? It means adults will trust you more when you follow the rules. They might even give you more freedom.

Why Are Rules Important?

Have you ever played a game where someone didn't follow the rules? That's no fun. Games have rules so everyone knows what to expect. That way you can play and have a good time. When people break rules, the game gets mixed up. People get upset. It makes things harder for everyone.

Rules are part of life for many of the same reasons. They help people get along. Rules help keep us safe and healthy too.

Rules Are Shared Agreements

Rules are usually shared agreements. The people in a community, or group, **agree** to follow them. That helps the people play, learn, or work together.

School rules help the classroom be safe, calm, and organized. That way everyone can learn and do their best.

You also have rules at home, like no eating in bed. These rules help adults take care of your family and your things. (And keep bugs out of your bed!)

Some rules are **laws**. Laws have to be followed by everyone, even adults. You might know some of these laws:

Green means go, and red means stop. Everyone everywhere knows those rules! Imagine how hard it would be to go anywhere without them.

What if you're in a new place with new people? It's still important to follow the rules. But how can you know the rules in a new place?

Start by being polite. Say please and thank you. Watch what everyone else is doing. If you're not sure about a rule, ask.

CHAPTER 2

Safety Rules

Some rules are meant to keep us **Safe**.

> Don't touch
> the stove.

There's a good reason for that rule. A hot stove can burn you.

Putting on your seatbelt is another rule that's meant to protect you. A seatbelt keeps you safer if there's an accident.

Lining up after recess helps teachers keep track of you. They don't want to lose you.

Watch Out for Ouches

Sometimes the reason for a safety rule isn't obvious. Some families have a rule that you have to clean your room. What's the point of that? After all, it's your room!

Cleaning your room is no fun. But neither is stepping on a toy or tripping over laundry. A clean room is a safer room.

You may not want to wear a hat and mittens when it's cold out. But your parent says you have to. There's a good reason for that rule. Winter gear keeps you from becoming an icicle and getting frostbite. (That really hurts!) You can stay warm while you make snowballs and have fun.

Putting on sunscreen might be a hassle. But it sure doesn't feel good to be cooked by the sun. Sunscreen protects you from sunburn.

Adults make safety rules because they care about you.

What's the Reason for the Rule?

You can tell a rule is meant to help keep you or someone else **safe** if . . .

- you could get hurt if you broke the rule
- it protects you from harm

And remember, **safety rules** *rule*!

CHAPTER 3

Healthy Body Rules

Some rules help you grow up healthy and strong. Just like vegetables, these rules are "good for you."

Take Care of Your Body

Your family might have rules about **food**. These rules help you learn to take care of your body.

Have you ever heard of a rule about *not* eating vegetables? Probably not. But maybe you have a rule that says you need to eat your veggies if you want dessert. Or a rule about not eating too many sweets. Chocolate cake tastes good, but too much can make you sick.

Many families have a rule about bedtime. It might be . . .

Lights out at
8:00.

Some nights you may not feel tired at 8:00. You may not agree with the rule those nights. But having a regular bedtime helps your body rest and get ready for the new day.

Did you know that kids need more sleep than pro athletes? It's true! You're still growing, and that takes extra energy. You need the energy that sleep gives you.

8:10

Many kids have to follow rules that limit **screen time**. That's because too much screen time can hurt your brain and your eyes. It keeps you from being active too.

Active? Yes! **Being active** is a big part of being healthy. It helps your bones, muscles, and brain develop. That's why playing outside and moving your whole body is important. Plus, it's fun!

What else is part of being healthy? Keeping clean.

You probably have rules about **keeping clean**. One might be that you have to brush your teeth every morning and every night. That's so you don't get cavities and don't have bad breath. Another might be about washing your hands after you go to the bathroom and before you eat. That helps stop the spread of germs. Germs can make you sick, so scrub up!

What's the Reason for the Rule?

You can tell a rule is meant to help you be healthy if . . .

- it helps you take care of your body
- it helps you get rid of germs

Healthy body rules help you feel good!

CHAPTER 4

Routine Rules

Rules are everywhere, for everyone, as part of every day. Some of these everyday rules help us get along with others. Some help us do what we need to do each day. And all of them help make every day the best it can be.

You can also think of these everyday rules as **routine rules**. They become routine when we do them automatically.

Here's a rule that should be automatic for all of us.

This rule helps us show **respect**. Respect is when you show someone that you think they are important. Their feelings matter. It's not only important to show others respect. It's important for others to show *you* respect. Feeling this respect makes every day go better.

All About Respect

How can you show respect to your friends?

Be kind. Be fair. Share your things, and don't hog the swings!

Share and take turns.

You can even show respect for your neighborhood. Put your garbage in the trash can and bottles and papers in the recycling bin every time. That's a routine rule that's good for all of us.

Work and Play and a Better Day

Do you have everyday rules that help make *your* day better?

Chores and homework first.
Play second.

You might want to play or read your favorite comic right after school. But getting chores and homework done first is important. After that you can do what you want. No worries about work waiting for you.

That's a nice routine!

Think about a part of your day that is hard. Maybe a new rule could help.

It can be frustrating if you can't find clean clothes or matching socks in the morning. Try laying out an outfit before going to bed. It will be ready in the morning. This can be your new routine rule!

What's the Reason for the Rule?

You can tell a rule helps with your routine if . . .

- it shows respect for someone
- it helps people get along
- it makes your day go better

Make the most of every day with **routine rules**.

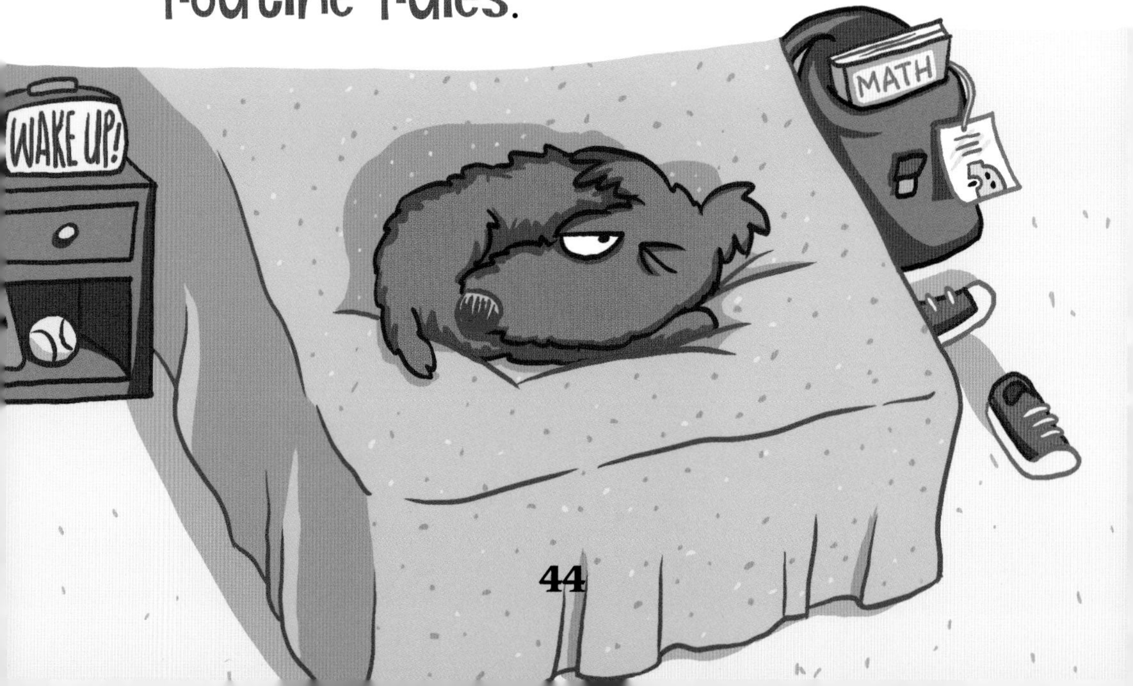

CHAPTER 5

"Just Because" Rules

You know those rules you hear over and over again? Those rules that seem like adults just want to boss you around? When you ask why, they might say, "Because I said so." How annoying!

Chew with your mouth closed.
Don't throw balls in the living room.

Turn off the lights.
Don't make the dog wear socks.

That bathroom rule is the worst. When you gotta go, you gotta go!

Why do adults have so many "just because" rules for kids?

It's not just to boss you around. (Okay, maybe sometimes.) Usually, these rules help keep things in order and make life easier for the group. They can help prevent something bad from happening.

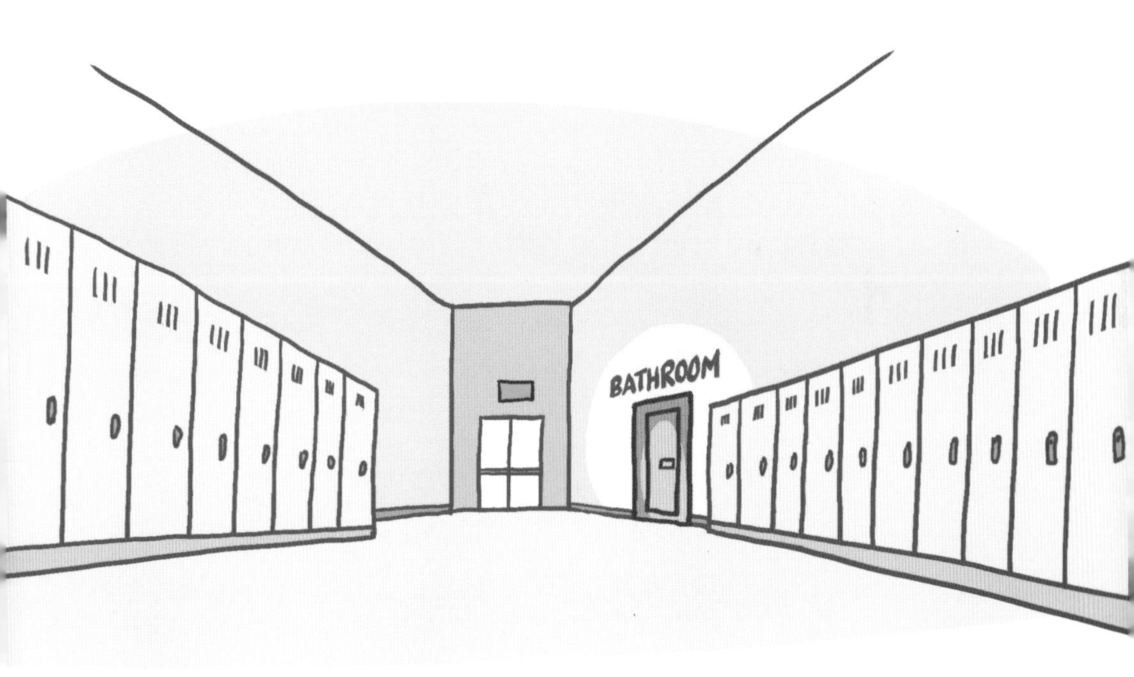

Why So Bossy?

When bossy rules bug you, try to remember that the adults in your life usually make rules for a reason. If you don't know what it is, you can ask:

"Why can't we play catch inside?"

The adult might say, "Because I said so." If that happens, ask a different question. Something like:

"How does this rule help you? And how does it help us?"

One Big Rule for Asking About Rules

Do you want to talk with an adult about the reasons for a rule? It's important to discuss it in a way that shows you really want to learn. Don't argue or act mad. The adult may be willing to talk about the rule if you show that you really want to understand.

The adult might agree to change the rule—or part of the rule. For example, maybe you can't throw the frisbee inside because you might break something. But you can toss the spongy ball.

What's the Reason for the Rule?

The adult might not have a good answer when you ask. Sometimes, even adults don't think very hard about their rules. It might be that "just because" is all you get. If that happens, you can ask yourself:

"How might following this rule help us all get along?"

That can make it a little bit easier to accept those bossy rules.

You know the rule: Close the fridge!

Exceptions to Rules

Sometimes things change, but rules stay the same. When you have a substitute teacher, you should still follow the classroom rules! Teachers and other students need to cooperate to have a good day.

Your teacher today:
Mr. Thompson

Other times, rules can change. It might depend on where you are or what's happening. It might depend on who you're with.

Let's say you're having lunch with your friends. They might not mind if you talk with your mouth full. But chances are that won't go over well with your family.

When Something Special Happens

Sometimes rules also change on special occasions.

Maybe your teacher shows up in a dinosaur costume. That's probably a good clue it's going to be a special day. The rules might be more relaxed. Holidays and your birthday are also special days when the rules might be less strict.

What are other **Special times** when the rules change? Do you get to stay up later on certain nights? Are there times you get to eat extra dessert?

When You Need to Be Safe

Rules can change if someone is hurt or in danger. When an emergency happens, don't worry about rules to be quiet or sit still. Let everyone know, and take action to be safe.

If you're about to throw up, get to a garbage can, quick! You don't need to raise your hand and wait your turn.

Is someone bothering or hurting you? Tell them no. Get away from them! Don't worry about rules for showing respect.

What's the Reason for the Exception?

Changes that are just for a while are called exceptions. It's okay to make an exception to a rule if something big is happening, like . . .

- a special occasion
- something is wrong
- someone is hurt or about to be hurt

Rules aren't meant to be broken. But there are **exceptions**!

Five Tips for Surviving the Rules

Life is better when you understand the reasons for rules. Your days are smoother. But sometimes it feels like too much. You might get frustrated when you hear a new rule or are told a rule you already know.

If you're feeling worried about surviving all the rules, turn the page. You'll find five tips to help.

Tips for Rules!
RULES
RULES
RULES

Tip 1: If You Don't Know the Rule, Ask

Sometimes you don't know the rules, or you don't understand them. When that happens, **look for clues**. You can watch to see how other people are behaving.

Ask questions if you need to. The people around you can probably help.

DO NOT TOUCH
DO NOT TOUCH
I'm sorry.

Tip 2: Apologize When You Need To

Sometimes people make mistakes. If that happens to you, don't worry. You're learning, and most people will understand. Mistakes are actually part of learning. The important thing is what you do next.

If you accidentally break a rule, **apologize** to the people it affects. That might be a parent, teacher, friend, or someone else.

Tip 3: Find a Way to Fix Things

Maybe you broke a rule, and something bad happened. Did you hurt someone or something? Did you lose a grown-up's trust?

Remember: Mistakes help us learn. But you still have to be responsible and tell the truth. And find out how you can **fix what you did**. It's all part of growing up.

(We all know it wasn't the cat who broke your mom's favorite mug!)

Tip 4: Forgive Someone Who Breaks a Rule

Sometimes, someone breaks a rule that's important to *you.* Maybe a friend breaks a rule in a game you play. Or they accidentally hurt your feelings.

When that happens, you may feel sad or angry. Ask the person what's going on. Maybe the rule needs to change. Or maybe they don't understand how important it is to you.

If the person apologizes, try to **forgive** them. Remember: Everyone makes mistakes.

Tip 5: Ask About Changing the Rule

Sometimes you might break a rule because you disagree with it or don't like it. That's a bigger mistake, because you knew better. Again, you will need to apologize. It's almost always best to obey a rule, even if you don't really want to.

But you can always ask about changing the rule. Remember to be respectful, just like when you ask about rules you don't understand (page 52). Show the adult that you care about the rules, and maybe some rules can be decided together. If the adult has a good reason for the rule, you may have to learn to accept it.

Now You Know the Reasons for Rules

When everyone knows and agrees on the reasons for rules, it's easier to follow them. It's easier to get along with other kids and adults—whew! That's always nice.

Knowing the reasons for rules helps you have the best day you can, every day.

If you were ruler, what rules would YOU make?

ENJOY YOUR DAY
PET AREA
WALK
DO NOT FEED THE DUCKS

GLOSSARY

affects: (page 71) makes something happen or makes someone feel a certain way

community: (page 10) a group of people who live together or do things together, like a family, classroom, school, team, or town

cooperate: (page 56) to work together on the same thing

exception: (page 64) when something is different from its usual way

independence: (page 7) being able to do things on your own

laws: (page 12) rules made by the government

polite: (page 14) well-behaved, like saying "please" and "thank you"

respect: (page 37) showing that you think someone is important and their feelings matter

routine: (page 34) things that you do pretty much the same way each time

strict: (page 60) when someone demands that rules are followed exactly

surviving: (page 66) continuing on when something is hard

About the Authors and Illustrator

Malcolm Munene and Kyra Ostendorf are a son and mother author pair living in Minneapolis. Malcolm is in high school; he plays soccer and Xbox and loves reading manga. Kyra cheers for the soccer team, doesn't play Xbox, and loves reading historical fiction. They had the idea to write this book together after a security guard at the mall said Malcolm and his friends had to leave. The mall had a rule that kids under age sixteen could not be there without an adult. Malcolm and his friends were behaving well, they were just too young! Kyra understood Malcolm's frustration, but as the mom, she said, "There are reasons for rules." They talked a bit about what those reasons might be, and then Kyra said *reasons for rules* could be a book. And Malcolm said, "Let's write it!" They believe that rules should be respected *and* questioned when they aren't fair. And they hope this book helps you the next time rules are frustrating.

Steve Mark is a freelance illustrator and a part-time puppeteer. He lives in Minnesota and is the father of three and the husband of one. Steve has illustrated many books for children, including *Ease the Tease!* and *Make a Friend, Be a Friend* from the Little Laugh & Learn® series and all the books in the Laugh & Learn® series for older kids.